T0209025

SWAGGGIN' HIP-HOP

Gentlemen Grinding & Gettin' It

D J R T H E M I

authorHOUSE®

AuthorHouse™
1663 Liberty Drive
Bloomington, IN 47403
www.authorhouse.com
Phone: 1 (800) 839-8640

This is a work of business. Names, characters, places and incidents are the product of the author's imagination to inspire. Any resemblance to actual persons living or dead, business establishments, events or locales is entirely coincidental.

Published by AuthorHouse 07/13/2016

ISBN: 978-1-5246-0744-9 (sc)
ISBN: 978-1-5246-0743-2 (e)

Print information available on the last page.

Any people depicted in stock imagery provided by Thinkstock are models, and such images are being used for illustrative purposes only. Certain stock imagery © Thinkstock.

This book is printed on acid-free paper.

Acknowledgments

To my Mother with Love, Honor and
Respect,

In Loving Memeory Of my Father with
Love, Honor and Respect(R.I.P.),

To my Son with Love, Honor
and Dedication for life,

To my beautiful and loving Wife

Contents

Introduction

There is many ways a story can be told, and many ways the game can be showed, but he who listen well, and apply will reap the benefits of paying close attention. The game pays whomever plays the game. This is a short story on business and great determination, that had to happen coming from my background of visionary hard workers. Without good work ethics nothing will happen, no matter how much someone wishes like hell for it to happen! I will not hold you long dear reader, from getting some strategies and game on business. This book will show you how, I started the business RT Hemi Entertainment, that has taken the South by a storm. It wasn't easy, and it damn sure wasn't hard either, but there are some major and serious principles that has to be strongly considered. Everyone that dreams of having major loot, normally don't have a plan. So as the saying goes, *"if you do not have a plan, then you are most surely planning to fail, and failing without planning it's not a plan or option if you desire to be successful."* In other words your actions are like a "hamster on a wheel." This destiny claimed me more than I desired it. Sometimes our dreams and goals gets detoured by some miraculous reasons that we sometimes don't understand at the time, but has time goes by, the plan starts to unfold its hidden destination for us. All humans have some kind of talent, but many of us fail to answer the call, or lack determination to stay focus, and follow the road that's been paved for us.

So, let me pull your coat to some game. As a great innovator and love in the game of Hip-Hop. Let me say this before I close this introduction, and I have said this many times, "The hardest part of the game is not starting, but staying on the track with discipline and strengthen, and only then will you see the results of your invested time. This music business, is my air, so it's my life!"

Fruits And The Tree

These young brothers came from a close net family. Their families was and is the back-bone of these young brothers' spirit and mind. DJ RT's family is a close family in many ways than most. DJ RT's mother is a very religious lady with strong morals and dignity. His father(R.I.P.) was a strong man with great work ethics, and always taught DJ RT and his siblings about work. There was a time when he stated that his father told him, "Boy if you don't work for anything don't expect to receive anything." DJ RT said his father didn't say much, but when he did, it made a lot of sense when he got older enough to understand. J-Boy's parents were rather young when they had him. J-Boy's father(R.I.P.) use to run the streets with DJ RT' s brother P. Los. DJ RT always looked at his brother P. Los for that game. But it took several of incidents in his young life before he would value the knowledge that would shine on him later. We will get into that much later in the book. J-Boy lost his parents while rather young, so his grandparents were forced to take the parent role. Plus, they were already his grandparents that just made it more official. J-Boy's grandmother was a quiet lady that was very devoted to her husband (R.I.P.) and grandchildren. She is a devout church lady and believer, and his grandfather was on the city council board. Between the city council and the church structure, J-Boy grew up with some political structure, and religious moral forms. DJ RT Hemi's mother would always put some type of church and family reunion functions together, and his father was a supervisor on his job. These young brothers grew up with some type of structure in their young lives. DJ RT grew up with five other sibling other than himself, and J-Boy had three other siblings. So looking at these brothers background you can see that they were destine for something great other than wasting their talents. The most shocking and elating part about all this, is even they didn't know until wisdom, and time would reveal to them their role they had to play. This path was carved out for these brothers because someone was paying close attention, and was able to recognize true talent. Knowing how to recognize rare and raw talent takes a very keen mind and eye. The best part about these guys talents, and dreams is there aspirations with great enthusiasm. DJ RT Hemi once said, "My brother P. Los told me you got to know when and how to use enthusiasms. It's very important in the game of business." This lesson became a great quality these brothers honed. Knowing how to use enthusiam and raw energy is what the hip-hop culture vibes from. Sitting with DJ RT one night he stated, "You can be the best rapper, and don't have that energy were your audience can't feel you. Sooner or later you will fall off. People just don't want to hear you, they got to feel you. That's what RT Hemi Entertainment gives the people, and that's why they want us. Good music and that raw gusty feeling that says hell yeah! You know what I mean?" You can fell DJ RT's vibe when you talk with him. I mean you can really feel this brother vibe and sincerity about what he does, and how he does it. This is a rare quality that most people fail to understand, but these brothers learned this quality from their family tree and surroundings. The tree that always gives fruits(seeds/kids) the time, love, heart, and attention with enthusiasm came from the old school parents that truly understood the vibe of love. Today it's material shit over human feelings! Not to say there is something wrong with giving or sharing with your loves ones, but to give of yourself is costly and rare today. The old school understood that giving your time and love would pay off. Most parents today are trying too much to live through their children that it creates too much conflict, because the child or children doesn't get to use their own minds. The old school would plant images and thoughts into the kids minds, and let the seed of thought germinate.

I remember one night while sitting in the barber-shop, DJ RT Hemi stated when I asked him about the kind of music he grew up listening to.

He replied, "I grew up listening to gospel because of my mother, country music because of my father. I got into hip-hop from my brother P. Los. I mean that cat had all kinds cassettes tapes of rappers in this milk crate. One of my older brother L-Lou had the R&B and Blues. So, I was always surrounded by music." J-Boy told me one night while chilling at their function that was greatly packed. I didn't think that I would get a chance to talk to him, but I caught up with him much later. He told me, "My father(R.I.P.) was strongly into hip-hop, and he would only listen to R&B when my T-Lady(R.I.P.) was around. I was young but I remember that much." So as the saying goes, <u>"The fruit definitely doesn't fall far from the tree, nor does the branches or leaves."</u>

Crime And Rhyme Pays

I got the news on the wire that these brothers were facings some illegal issues, but that didn't stop these brothers. The next day when the brothers were clear and handle those illegal issues, DJ RT Hemi and J-Boy, I asked them how this happen. J-Boy stated, "I guess being young and dumb?" Then I asked DJ RT Hemi, "Being dumb and trying to move too fast without looking at the game from all angles."

I caught up with these brothers a week later. I asked, "So what do you guys have planned next?" DJ RT Hemi commented, "I don't know right now. To keep living and learning, and taking care of my kid for me is one of the major moves, being a devoted husband and also help my T-Lady." Then I asked J-Boy, "What's your next move? He looked at his cell-phone then replied, "Get my shit together. I didn't come into this world to be a loser! I have a mission, but I don't know what it is right now. You keep interviewing and following Us, and you will see the mission. It's in the making I know that for sure!" They both walked off, then DJ RT Hemi asked me, "How did you know we had faced some legal issues?" I grinned and told him, "Much later I will reveal it to you, but right now I can't. Is that fair?" RT replied, "Well it has to be since you say you will reveal it to me much later, and I definitely would like to know. I don't like people following me without giving me the scoop on why!"

After about two or three weeks later I caught DJ RT in the barber-shop again. I didn't ask him anything I just wanted to see and hear what he had to say. The Barber "Skip" asked DJ RT a question, and I never will forget the look on his face. At this point, I knew this was the turning point for DJ RT. Skip "The Barber" asked him, "Hi, you haven't got any of that Light from that brother yet, huh?" RT replied, "From who?" Then Skip smiled and said, "From that brother P. Los. Man you better get some of that! I'm telling you brother. You don't find too many brothers with that kind of knowledge, and the way he gives it to you. The brother is deep! I have seen many cats come into this shop and talk that talk. I have seen him and a few brothers debate, and that brother would shut them niggas down. Even to this day nobody will ask that brother anything about religion, politics and philosophy." DJ RT was silent while Skip and me started chopping it up as the saying goes. When DJ RT was through getting his fade. I asked him could I have a few words with him and ask a few questions, but he just kept it moving. I knew that was a very deep question, and a lot came with that question. That was a very heavy question for a young man's mind to bare, and shoulders to carry. DJ RT isn't the ordinary kind of guy. You will see why I can make a statement like this much later. The more I was around these guys, the more I saw their minds started to grasp their mission, meaning and purpose. Most people fail to understand the power of questioning the mind. That's the way the mind works. When you question the mind you put it to work. This is a great quality of mental discipline these brothers grew up on. They didn't know they possessed this artful mental quality at that time. Like I said, time is the essence of life that reveals the big picture. The old saying goes, "*a picture is worth a thousand words that feeds great minds.*" These brothers had a thousand and one words. They didn't boast about what they did; they would let their work and actions speak for itself. Even to this, day these brothers has surprised a lot of people. Especially them haters! DJ RT Hemi replied one night when some stupid cats were getting into a squabbling match, they were forced to pack up and the function was over. He stated, "Haters are blockers that give you more drive to finish, and they are like dirt to plants. Without dirt the plants can't grow, and the same way with me. I grow from their negative dirt that I use like fertilizer. So as long as they tell me no, that inspires me to say yes." When these brother of DJ RT Hemi Entertainment were facing illegal issues, that incident could have broken a destiny for this great pair. One could have lied or ratted on the other for a quick release, or to remove a stain from their record. Thes guys stayed true to the code. Which is taking your rap sheet like the street solider suppose to. DJ RT made a comment about crime. He stated, "I know I said this before, but I'm said it again, that crimes pays the other man, but it pays me in another form and fashion. Because now its part of my tactical mindset, my grind and how use this art of music. It also shapes my game, and reality to be that much sharper, about who I can kick it with. Are they down for me, or are they acting like they down with me just to come up off my plans and dreams. You got to ask yourself some times these questions. For my man J-Boy he showed me he is down. You can't buy loyalty. Because loyalty has to be earned like love, but its much deeper. That was a great listen that taught me that crime is not for me. I have witnessed a lot of cats, get thrown into the can for years for doing petty shit. I learned that from my blood brother and by my mistakes. So crime can create rhymes and a creative mind. Rhymes can pay and being a great DJ is my stake, for real." DJ RT always keeps it moving with a purpose and reason to fulfill his mission. One thing I know, and two things for certainty. One, when something is in your blood you can not change what's in your blood, and two DJ RT grew up around music, great work ethics, being organized, and knowing that you have a purpose and mission that has to be fulfilled. You can see this deep within DJ RT's DNA. Every positive action has a negative reaction behind the veil and vise versa. One of the major things that stuck with these innovators for years is their undying determination to reach another level in the game of life. They always turned their negative to a positive, like night turns or becomes into day. As these young brothers began to grow more with time, and their dreams and minds were developing with a vision. You would come to the conclusion that these are some driven young men. They pay close attention to things around them. These guys wanted to be somebody, and not just a fucking banal nobodies. As these guys were mentally and physically growing up into age of men, mind and purpose for sure. They were looking at trends, observing the times, questioning themselves and the world around them. They knew when they graduated from high school they definitely needed to have their shit together. These brothers were swaggging like normal hood cats. They were hungry for something that would give them that edge of life, that spelled "$uccess!" These brothers didn't let anything stop them. Even if something had the potential and ability to slow them down or stop them. They did not give in! DJ RT said to me one night, "My brother told me! Look here, I mean he was serious. You have to know when someone is talking to you or with you, and my brother P. Los always chopped up with me and for me. You know what I mean? He said look, 'it's two eyes, one mind, an undying spirit of action that makes one vision clear with purpose, meaning, and reasons to be successful.' That's why the RT Hemi Entertainment are still swaggging like real swagggers swaggg, for that that green bag, that makes a large stash."

His Idea But My Game

There was a time when DJ RT Hemi's brother L-Lou would DJ for the local rodeos. This went on for months and months, and maybe years. Lou, RT's brother would always ask people if they had this music or that music, and he knew they didn't because they didn't love music like him. Plus, as the DJ that was his responsibility to have all the variety of music to keep the people dancing and happy. Lou loved music, but don't get me wrong. Their was a difference from the way Lou loved music, than his little brother DJ RT loved music.

One day I got the wire that these brothers were deejaying for a local party, and the following week they were doing another local party. RT Hemi made this statement, "Doing local parties is how I got my start. Then I was approached to do a Rep your Hood Party at a place called the C-Lounge. It's a local place, but that night it showed me a lot. For instance, taking personal requests, watching how people can act with one another, observing how certain music creates a certain vibe, and how to keep the people happy. This was my debut for my destiny. That same night I couldn't sleep. I was so inspired. I started using my brothers equipment. We would argue about it, but then I came up with a plan. I would pay him a little something to keep me going until I got my own shit." There is one thing about business that most people that do not have a business probably will never understand. That in order to have a business, you must invest money, time, energy, mind, planning, and a passion to never give up. Most people quit before they start. Failure is not an option or hinderance, it's a reason to keep going and learning until one day you start earning." When these brothers started doing their thing the word was getting around about these brothers. There were older cats that were in the same business would ask questions about these young brothers, concerning their equipment, parties, admission, bookings, and different places they were traveling. These guys was so focused, and they knew how the crowd would react when they played. They were among the in-crowd at a time themselves. One guy that would hook up with these brothers would fall off later, so that made another change with a little diverse business interest. I will not mention this guy's name to protect the inoccent. But this guy's lack of focus was a blessing in the disguised. From that point on these brothers were official business men. As the word was getting around, and these brothers were using the social media for advertising and word of mouth. They were not getting what they were hungry for at the time, but they kept it moving like a shark eating all fish in their proximity and they have to, in order to survive. If a shark don't keep moving it will die. These brothers were doing the same thing to other local DJs, booking all the local functions to stay a alive. They were eating up all the local competition and out swaggging the other DJs. They were doing graduation parties, family reunions, kids parties, church functions. I was surprised when I saw on the media page, that these brothers were deejaying for a church gathering. This function was booked by an elderly lady. They were giving this lady her 93rd birthday party, and nominating her for being a member of the church board for over 40 years. When I showed up at the function. I asked DJ RT Hemi about doing this type of function. He was like, "There's some things you have to do, and there is also some things you must do in this business. You got to be diverse and versatile to accommodate all your potential customers. When you are in this business you can't say, well I'm just going to play this type of music or just play for this group of people when you are starting out. You better have a another gig, because this type of gig pays as you play. If you are playing then you are getting paid. If you read my business cards. What does it say, _I do it all_! So that's why I'm here. These nice peope got the word from another family member, and that was weeks ago. All they want to hear is Blues, and Gospel. They don't want me to play no Hip-hop or club music. I was like, they are paying, and that's what I'm playing. I remember before I was a DJ there was this DJ, and he was arguing with the people about the music he wasn't going to play. How do you think that played out? He doesn't DJ no more from what I have heard, and plus I haven't seen him. I'm not going to mention his name." These brothers understood what it took for them to reach another level in this game. Your name has to be on people minds, and the people that's hiring you for a function has to know that you are reliable by all means. DJ RT Hemi would always say, "If you are not taking care of your business, that means that you don't have no business, and if you don't have no business, then you are taking care of somebody else's business, or you are dipping into another person's business. That's a bad label to have, because your are labeled a hater, and no one wants to be a hater. Some haters don't even know that they are hating. When you don't support people, when they need your support, and knowing you can help and you don't, that's envy and hatered. When you DJ for some people, and they give you all these lies and excuses about why they can't pay you, that's a another form of hatred." These brothers were passing out business cards, using the social media, making calls, and word of mouth was their forms of best advertising. J-Boy one day was with his daughter when I approached him about the Hemi Entertainment, "We are on the rise surely. We have a support system that many don't know about, and that's a good thing. Because niggas out here are stuck on stupidity. I'm not talking about those that support Us. They know who they are, but like the boy RT Hemi say, 'Haters are my motivators, so you got to love them for the negative shit.' Then he drove off. I didn't get a chance to ask another question, but I'm sure I would get another chance later and I did as usual.

Later that same day, I caught up with the RT Entertainment they were packed with their equipment, and were fixing to hit the road again. DJ RT Hemi was behind the wheel. I asked where they were headed. He replied "This time we are on our way to a town in the deep south, we call it the "Sticks." I'm leave you with this one. "This was my brother's idea to start Deejaying, but since I got started I always felt like this was my game, Dig?

I will get at you later. You keep interviewing us, and I guarantee it will pay off later. We Swagggin." Then the brothers jetted off with a smile on their faces, that facial glare still gives me the chills about success till this very day. If you are not inspired, then you will not inquire, which is the fuel for a successful life with a great desire.

Triple L's

Three weeks went by, and I haven't heard nothing about the RT Hemi Entertainment having any type of functioning going on. That was kind of odd. For something like this to go on for weeks, when these brothers were doing their thing weeks after weeks for months on a continuous bases. I checked their media site to see if anything was going on, and there was nothing planned or scheduled. So, I got up and went to the Mall to get me a pair of fresh jeans and a shirt for the Brother and Sisterhood Yearly Picnic. When I was coming out of one of the stores, and you would not have guessed who I saw to my surprise. It was DJ RT Hemi with his son. When I called his name I notice a few young college, or High School looking students ran over to were DJ RT Hemi and his son were standing. It was about four girls and three boys. So I walked over where they were standing, and a girl asked DJ RT, if he was the RT Hemi that put her best friend's graduation party together at the local C-Center on the North-west side of the city. DJ RT replied he did. He signed a few T-shirts for them and passed out a few business cards. We greeted each other with that hood embracement. He ordered some food for his son, while him and I was chopping it up. I asked, "I've been waiting on another function from you, but to my dismay I have not heard or seen anything. What's going on?" He said, "I don't know what's really going on. It's like everything came to a stand still. Honestly that shit don't sit well with me." Then he stated," Come to the barber shop later on about 7pm, and we'll take it from there about our next move." I told him I would catch up with him later. After I

12

attended the brother and sisters' yearly gathering of playing several games of chess, smoking cigars and being sociable. I dropped my fiancée off at home. I continued on my journey to the barber-shop. I was very excited and eager to see what DJ RT had planned. When I turned down the street that led to the barber-shop. Cars were parked all along side the street that lead up to a large gathering of people having a good time, music blasting, the barbecue pit was smoking, a large deep fish fryer was lit up, and large coolers of soda, beer and water. There was lounging chairs, two tables of dominoes was set up for the women and men playing bones. After walking a great distance, and reaching the circle of fun. DJ RT and my eyes connected, and that big grin of progress of hustling with a plan came across DJ RT Hemi's face. I walked to the DJ booth. We embraced. The first thing he hit me with was, "My brother P. Los told something, and it hit me when I left the Mall. He told me always perform the triple L's." I asked, "What are the triple L's?" He stated, "Looking, listening and learning. Always be looking to see what the people are doing, then listen to what they want, and finally, learn how to supply what they want. See sometime people be wanting to have a good time, but they don't always have the money to do it. So I figured, I would do something for them on me, and that way I will be getting them back into the mood of partying, because if they are not partying I'm not deejaying. Another thing my brother told me was, and this keeps me going. If you read about business you will keep your mind on business, and when you are doing something to stay in business, then you will have a business, and mainly it's your business to handle your business. So, if you handle the business that you love doing, then you will always be doing the thing you love doing, which is being in business. Plus, this way people don't get to complacent. You got to keep your people in the mood, so they can keep you in the groove. There are many things about people that my brother told me that came to my thoughts, and I have to start using them. Anyway, falling into this temporary slump was a great lesson." I looked at this guy, and I'm thinking this guy used to be kind of quiet, but it just confirms what I said before. When you grow mentally, you grow spiritually, and when you are spiritually fed by your passion, then you become an asset of action. I asked, "You really look up to your brother?"

He replied, "Isn't that what big brothers suppose to do? That brother taught me a lot about business, people and the world. These lessons has much weight to them. One day I'm hook you up, so the both of you can chop it up. When it happens I bet $100 you will walk away spellbound." We were at the DJ booth, and DJ RT Hemi instantly played another song. When DJ RT put that track on, the domino game just stopped, and people got up and started dancing as if they were inside the club. They started "screaming go Hemi, go Hemi!" We were outside in a empty lot next to the barber-shop. I thought to myself damn this guy P. Los. I was anxious to met this guy. Wow! Those triple L's. I guess I will have to start looking at life and people with that triple L perspective. This guy DJ RT Hemi came up with a plan in just a few hours. I figure if it works for these Brothers, it damn sure can work for me. After playing a game of chess with Skip "The Barber", and then I said my good-byes to RT Hemi. I was on my way back home, and my mind way reeling back my day of kicking it with RT Hemi Entertainment again. These cats never has given me a dull moment whenever I've talk with them. The more I talk with these guys, the more I was learning something about me, and what I can do to start some type of business for my peeps and me.

One thing that Blacks or African-Americans need is a place for entertainment. We can have that only if we stop acting like damn fools, and be the people we really are. Cool dudes with a swagger that's truly smooth and true to the hood and crew. That's a little something the RT Hemi Entertainment engraved within my conscious every time I see or think of them. These cats are innovators in every sense and letter of the word. Come to think about it. I'm doing exactly what DJ RT Hemi has learned. The triple L's of life. I'm looking at these brothers work ethics, listening to their business savvy, and learning about the dedication of doing business, and supplying the people what they want. One thing that comes to mind is what DJ RT Hemi said, "Having a business, doing business, and staying in business is not for the timid. The booking has to be on point. You have to be a reliable asset for your clientele, and the triple L's helps every time."

The Connection

I was at my computer, when I received a phone call from one of my best female-friends. She wanted me to come by, and talk with a few sisters and brothers concerning the lessons on the importance of economics, obligations of men and women, importance of family values, education, and the responsibility to the church. After conversing with the brothers and sisters, I was called by one of my seminar business associate. I met this gentlemen at a business seminar years ago, and from that point on we stayed in touch with one another much as possible. Due to his busy construction company, that would force him to travel to other towns and cities, and me with my strong desire to become a serious prolific writer. We always made time to converse about life, people, business, money, spiritual devotion and family. I went by his home as usual. We sat outside having our usual intellectual conversation about the responsibilities of the Elders and the responsibility of the young adults, which forces us to have a better community and economical lifestyle. These responsibilities range from the spiritual, moral, political, economic, family, society, education and community. That places us in a ethnic dilemma! Needing more young minds that desire to know, and fulfill their moral responsibility to our ancestors is the great missing piece to the puzzle. This distinguish gentlemen was from a mix ethnic family. His father was an African-American and his mother was a Caucasian! I was conversing with a brother from both sides of the ethic fence concerning our great reasonability, that cause us to be morally and spiritually irresponsible to one another. One would be amazed from the expensive paintings that he had of the Moors in Spain on his wall. He held Africans in great regard for the lessons they brought to Europe, these were African Wise Men and Warriors. This Elderly brother had always welcomed me into his home like one of the family. He was an elderly well respected individual by all means. When I left his home after about three hours. Which was partaking of a hot delicious vegetable soup, smoking cigars, drinking on some imported wine and also partaking in a few games of chess. I could tell that my mentor wasn't the same, and I would find out later why my elderly mentor was putting things in order with a strong conviction with me playing a major part. When I made it home, I had received another call from one of my B.Y. E. Brothers concerning DJ RT Hemi. He told me that the brother wanted to get some knowledge, to receive some Light. I wanted to know where this would take place. I finally made that connection. I met DJ RT Hemi's brother P. Los, and he was definitely on point! This brother was heavy concerning a wide range of topics. When DJ RT Hemi and me left his brother's home. Who was a B.Y. E. Brethren that I had finally had the chance to meet, and he also was a brethren of the Ancient Mystic Ausarian Order.

DJ RT Hemi told me, when we stopped for a few drinks at this sports bar. He said, "One day my brother P. Los, had took me to this big elegant white house with great brick-masonry architecture. It was a suburban area with a well secure community with iron and brick fences that surrounded all these big two and three story homes. We pulled in this driveway, and their was a large white 4-door Ford F-150. When my brother ranged the doorbell I was a little nervous. This white-man, that appeared to have some Black in him, had this dark tan hue. He was a elderly looking man, but very respectable. We spoke and my brother introduced me, and we went into this large study. There was a painting of a black warrior on the wall, I was shocked! This guy asked, did I want to be a businessman, because my brother had told him about me. This guy said,…huh now I'm try to remember this, but he went right to the point." Then a waitress came asking if we were ready to order. We ordered a thing of hot wings and two beers, while sitting in this sports bar. Then DJ RT Hemi continued telling me about his connection that really put the icing on the cake. I asked, "What was the guy's name?" He stated, "I'm not going to mention his name, because the lesson is more important." I agreed. Then he continued with his story. He said, "The guy asked if I wanted be a business man. I told him yes. Then he asked, if I was doing what I loved doing. I told him yes! Shit because I do! Now I didn't use that type of language around him. That old guy hit me like this, 'if you love doing what you do, and willing to go a step further like your brother, you will be in business one day. I didn't put money in your brother's hand. Your brother found a way to finance his own books. See your brother loves to write, and I told him, if you love writing, then get off your ass and write, and the money will come to finance your next project. Sure I could have giving him the money. He being a brother and a very serious brother. He did what he had to do. First, you have to make some great adjustments, and cut out all the bullshitting! I will give you the things you need to take your deejaying business to, huh…how you youngsters say it? Take it to another level.' We all started laughing. 'Then he said I've been around.' "Moments later this lady walked in, and we all spoke. She introduced herself as the wife. She looked much younger than he did, but I wasn't there for that. Then she left out the room, and this guy continued." 'If you change the way you think, and see your business like you see the way you need air to breathe, then you will be successful! Hell maybe one day you will be one of the most successful persons that ever was a DJ. Plus, with deejaying skills you can even become a music producer, and that's more money. Remember money is only powerful when you know how to keep it, use it, and most all invest it. Now I'm willing to do some things for you, because I love to see young men be productive. Now, them damn fools robbing and stealing from one another, that's ignorance! But unfortunately, there are people like that in this world. Being a lazy young man will never get you anywhere, but on the corner with a beggars' cup. Now understand this, and I'm finish this subject before you gentlemen get back. If you sit with your brother, and learn what needs to be learned. I will help you, but I will not put money in your pocket, but I will help you whenever you have questions, and I mean I will show you how to put money in your pockets. The first steps will be the hardest, but the most necessary task to fulfill your purpose and goal. If you do this for about three months on a continuous bases. I guarantee you, that your business and your whole life will change. I'm leave you with that responsibility, and your brother's knowledge to guide you when you need it. Plus, come by any time, but call first. I mean call your brother first, then he will call me. Then we will take it from there, alright?' I said, "Yes, sir." Then he continued, 'I know you call him P. Los, but the brothers know him by another name, and I have to catch myself when other people are around. I don't want to get them mixed up, or have a misunderstanding. Anyway, if you do that. Then you will forever be welcomed to my home. I do not discriminate has you can see. I love helping! I donate to different charities. I also donated to different hospitals, universities and colleges.' I interjected, "Man DJ RT Hemi that was very profound. It's like being at the right place at the right time." He looked at me and replied, "Tell me about it. That guy turned my whole life around, and looking at business totally different. I mean three-hundred and sixty degrees around. From that little time that I spent there talking with that old man. His home showed me he knew what it was talking about, and I see why my brother lives in a nice neighborhood too. After making that connection, and spending more time doing what I was told and what was asked of me, I was all about my business. With my brother always in my ear, looking, listening, and learning. I knew and felt it. I'm taking RT Hemi Entertainment to another level! When I got back that night. I hit my boy and business partner J-Boy up. We talked like we never talked before about the future, and business plans for RT Hemi Entertainment plans for the future. I am amped up, keyed up, and definitely inspired. Plus, having a kid made it that much official to take care of my business. As the old adage goes, <u>"There's a time to work and a time to play. There is a time to sleep, and there is a time work. There is time for the family, and time for the business, but no time for bullshitting,</u> and as my brother would always say, there's never time for jaw-jacking when you can be paper-stacking, and being on your job career acting." I was spellbound from this interview. I didn't want to leave, because there was more I could have learned. But we had to leave, and plus DJ RT was all about the business. You could see that fire in his eyes. Like he would say at times, "If I'm not swagggin' then I'm draggin, and that definitely isn't the happenings!" So the connection was made for the RT Hemi Entertainment to take their label, their name in the game, and their dreams to another level.

F Jaw-Jacking, It's Paper Stacking

The Hemi Entertainment were doing there thing. They stayed on the move. These brothers were deejaying in different towns and cities that already had DJs, but they were persistent about handling their business. From the last conversation that I had with DJ RT Hemi at the sports bar, and he said I quote, 'I'm keyed up, amped up and inspired.' It was that noticeable about these guys determination to make a name in this game. They loved this game, and they aimed to please their clientele from town to town, and city to city. This type of shit made you think, *"do these guys ever get any rest or sleep?"* From the way they were constantly on the move you wouldn't think so. It got to the point that all you had to do was ask someone where the Hemi Entertainment were deejaying. I promise you! Someone had the scoop on the place and time. I remember one night J-Boy said, "Some times I get so inspired to book the next function, while we were deejaying that same night. Shit I would step outside and make a few phone calls. Knowing that the spots I'm calling are playing music from the juke box, and they probably are fucked up. What most people don't understand is that money is motivating. My nigga RT, man that nigga is serious about his money grind. Some time he would be like my brother P. Los said whop, whop, and I be like damn that nigga pretty sharp. That shit rubs off on you, then I rub it back on him, and that's what we do. We keep each other fed. One night I was wrapping a little too much with cats, and I was feeling good you know, fucking with that drink. My nigga came over, and said, 'it's okay to mingle and feel the crowd, but too much jaw-jacking fucks with your mind and hinders your grind for paper stacking.' That's my nigga he set me straight, and from that point on. I be mingling and feeling the crowd, but not forgetting what this shit is all about. It's about giving the people good music and having a fucking good time! Plus, all this shit we have to put up with as Black people, we need to have a spot to have a good time. You always got some damn fool that will fuck it up for the rest of us, that want to have a spot to enjoy ourselves and also have a good time." From that conversation with J-Boy you can feel the frustration when RT Hemi Entertainment couldn't do their thing. I remember RT Hemi and me were talking about the business getting their own spot or finding a permanent spot. He remarks were, "It's hard to find your own spot or should I say keeping your own spot. Because many people from different cities and towns are calling and needing you. So you got to move, and I'm going to move to where they need me. I like moving and getting down at different spots, and doing my thing. Man that's love! When you are very eager to do something, and some people don't understand that love you have for doing what you love doing. Some bring that bullshit, and it fucks with you! It does make you want to just put your foot in their hating and damn fool asses. Sometime you feel like just slapping some sense in him or her for their stupidity. Violence isn't the answer when it comes to doing what you do. You are in a high volume of different minds, different emotions, and on top of that many come with frustrations mixed with drinking. Now, that's when you have to be aware, and use the music to change that person or people moods. Learning how to use music to change people moods is an art within it self. It has to be learned for the betterment of the innocent that comes out to party and have a good time. This is what the RT Hemi Entertainment always trying to do, but people are going to be people. When emotions and frustrations fly, you got to try and calm the people down before it gets too heated, and this is the part I do not like. When some fool crashes the party, and kill the vibe because he or she is fucked up or just acting a damn fool! Plus, that makes you reconsider about having your own personal spot. They come with bullshit whether you got security or not. Then that forces the city to come shut you down, because you are getting too many calls about fights, people getting shot or whatever. That fucks with your business. We are trying to do business to stay in business to have a business, and give the people what they want. Most of all teach our kids about being productive, and doing something they love doing, which gives meaning and direction to their young lives. Also we want to teach them about the importance of paper stacking, and stay away from jaw-jacking."

These brother were growing in this business. Their name was ringing in the South from mouth to ear, and on the media sites. They are live as an electrical wire with 1000s of volts running through the electrical lines. They would fire up any town or city with good music and making people feel that party Swaggg vibe.

Love The Game

DJ RT Hemi, "If you not loving what you are doing, then you are not doing the thing you suppose to be doing. Shit the most important thing about loving what you are doing, is also doing it well. I don't know how many times I can say it. The more I do this shit the more it grows on me. I'm becoming it, and it's becoming me. Man I can't part with this shit. You hear me? That's why I came up with that motto and name. Hemi, it's way of saying you '<u>hear me</u>" in code, and street lingo. Like my brother P. Los would say you dig?" When RT Hemi graduated from high school. He went to a Technology School to further his education. He and I had a short conversation about schooling and this was his response. "When I graduated, I had to make up my mind on what I was going to do for the rest of my life. Either I was going to work for someone all my life, or was I going to invest into this Free-Market of Enterprising. So, what I did was move in with my brother P.Los, and went to Tech School. I got that trade or schooling. While I was attending classes I was working for the large corporate company that sold soft-drinks. Man them was some long hours, and hard work on my mind more than the physical. If it fucks with your mind then it's fucking with your body! While living with my brother I was talking with him, and my brother is the kind of cat to make you think and get deep within your mind. So he was getting at me. Not telling what to do! He was making me use my mind to see more options, and weigh my options with discriminatory decisions. One thing he said to me still sticks with me among the shit he enlighten me on. If you know how to use your mind and use your mind well, then you will understand how to use another person's mind to create ideas, see and hear options and see the power of creative thoughts working greatly that sharpens your skull. Damn that's deep! So I hooked up with this cat that was going to the community college for musical engineering. He told me one day to meet him at the campus about 8pm that night, and he was showing me different things dealing with the mixer, the voice structuring, about the microphones on why and what. Plus, he also needed the time for his grade, but I also had to pay. The school was just charging $25 an hour. That worked for me. I was able to learn this game, and do something with those studio ideas that was always tugging at my psychological business ideas. Those ideas have always kind of stuck with me. I didn't pursue it early. I guess it had to manifest within me. When I graduated from technology school, and they didn't help me find a job like they promised they would. I was like ok, What's next?" RT Hemi didn't know really how to answer that call at the time. What he was going through is what majority of us go through. It is called finding Self, and answering the call that will give meaning, and direction to one's life.

He continued, "After I moved out from staying with my brother I started chilling with my relative Slim. We were living the life of the party. I started working at this grocery store, and that was a laid back gig. I liked that shit, but it really wasn't paying shit. Plus, I didn't have any major bills. I put money in Slim' s hand for living with him. I know I can't live nowhere for free. I did what I suppose to do, and that is pay my way. My brother P.Los would come over and kick it with us, and you know before he would leave. He would always hit Slim and me with some spell- bound deep thinking. Later Slim, and me would converse about that deep shit, until we came up with some type of conclusion. (Later Slim and my brother, wouldn't be tight anymore.) The only thing my brother ever said about that was, 'Some people really don't know what loyalty and blood-ties really mean.' So I moved back home when my Old-man was getting sick, that way I could help him and the T-Lady out. Having a son even push me even more to come up with a serious gig. Because pampers and milk are not cheap!!! Then I started working for corporate warehouse. They were letting me move up, and get a little more, but that still didn't answer what

I was looking for. That's when I started talking with my brother P.Los and Skip "The Barber" more and more.

They are much older than me." This would be the unseen move at the time that DJ RT Hemi would make. These moves were shaping him, and his world around him to give the necessary tools to be operative, since his brother was giving him the speculative mind. His other brother was a contract-truck-driver. At the time making good money, and moving his truck when the money was good, was another thought that hit him. I asked RT Hemi about this brothers he didn't mention as much, and his response was, "Well me and my brother P.Los are closer, not to say me and my other brothers are not close because we are. My other brothers would talk at you or to you, but my brother P.Los, that cat would talk with you, and then leave you with all kinds of thoughts and ideas about your next move. He just has a way of getting with you, and on the slick-shit that make you think about reaching another level of this game. To me that's some slick shit. He was a hustler, and he is very calculative type of person, when it comes to seeing the weakness and talents in people. To him opportunities come from all kinds of people at different times. So I understood that, and from getting that understanding and learning much more about people and business. I had to re-educated myself to always be ready, and recognize an opportunity when it knocked or opened its door."

J-Boy and RT Hemi was classmates in high school, so they were hanging out more. J-Boy couldn't find that right person that was on his level while RT Hemi was living with his brother. When RT Hemi move back into the town that connection was in the mix. The more they started hanging with each other, and chopping it up about them being young fathers, helping the family, and trying to find a way to invest in the money system, instead being property of the industrial prison system. They would finally make that move one day. The C-Lounge, I know I have mentioned it before. This is a point I'm driving home about the love of this game, and loving what you are doing. When you love something, you will pursue it until it becomes yours "by all any means." There is a saying that P.Los would always say, when I interviewed him with RT Hemi. That saying was, _"If you are playing for keeps, then the thing or person your are playing to_

keep will always be kept. If you are not playing for keeps, then do not expect that
thing or person to be kept."

Since these guys has love for this game, and so much of it compels them to keep pursing and moving in that direction. That's thing about loving something or some one, you keep doing what it takes to posses it. Sometimes we love something that doesn't love us back the way we think it should be loving us. Sometimes we forget, and should question ourselves, *"Is it them or me, or maybe it's not meant to be?"* You will know because if its loving you back, it will still measure up to your level in some form or fashion. Only a damn fool would remain into something that doesn't measure up to their standard in some form or fashion. One thing that is certain to happen whenever you attend a business class, a business seminar or when it just comes to business. Mentors has always told their protégés, *"Do something that you love doing, that way you don't get completely cheated for your time and effort."* When you do what you love, you get twice the pay, and some times a life time of recompenses for your hard work. If you don't like what you are doing, there are many unseen serious issues that will occur, like health problems, a negative attitude can and will become a violent person when acted on, verbal attacks will be spoken to love ones, and all the positive doors will be closed because the mind is shut down from the lack of not feeling worthy of self. Love what you are doing, if not use it, but never let it use you. That's why the Hemi Entertainment are still swagging in this game of Deejaying. Honing their skills in the studios, *and learning to do business, to have a business, to be in business, and taking care of your business is the most important way to mind your own business to elevate in the business.* RT Hemi said this one night after a function. "I really dig Teddy Pendergrass, but that song "When Somebody Loves You Back." Now that song I use that song for a mental theme. Mr. Teddy Pendergrass(R.I.P.), that man was a genius! Mr. Pendergrass sung that part, *'Feel so good loving somebody when somebody loves you back.'* I say, It feels good loving this game, and when this game loves us back."

Hemi Entertainment Comes Alive

Hemi Entertainment was making bold business moves. They were knocking down all competition when it came to deejaying. They were called to perform in various places from Friday night to Sunday night. The word was spreading that Hemi Entertainment knows how to party and bring a crowd. It's the music that's being played, and it's the chemistry these cats bring to every function. Hip-Hop has a certain culture and mechanism that you have to possess, in order for whomever that steps in this circle, must know how to use it to become successful. Entering the business of hip-hop, you must understand the chemistry, the culture, the people, the music and the times to be successful. One major thing that many people, mainly artists and musicians also brings is culture trends. Hemi Entertainment understood this part of the game. They were called to perform in various places and clubs throughout the South. These brothers were moving around like a clock hands moves to the right. I caught RT Hemi one Sunday even coming out of electronic-store, and I was very surprised. We stood outside chopping it up in the parking lot. You know me, I had to pop them questions. "So what's happening and where's the next function? I like that energy that he always brings to a function, I stated." RT Hemi replied, "Right, we are putting various projects and functions together, for real! I mean some real functions. We going take this shit to the next level, for real! Like I told you before keep watching. You might learn a thing or two if you have not already." Then RT split the scene on me. I always get that surge of energy whenever I talk with that

Brother. That brother always has his mind on business for surety. That's the most important part of business is to have the mindset with certain actions that has to be carried out. Marketing was another aspect that DJ RT was focusing on, which is a major part of the business, in order for the business or any business for that matter to flourish. There has been a few times when Hemi Entertainment were asked by other local DJs that were trying to rise through the cracks, if they could ride or do something together one night, and could they get Hemi Entertainment input or use their name for the game. He stated, "I don't mind helping another brother, if we both came up with something, but I'm not going to help another person win to where I lose or help that person beat me out. When it's about competition to a certain degree. We can help bring the best out in each other. Hell yes! I'm for making or helping someone that wants to be better. I'm not going to give you the shovel to burying me in my own game. Like I said before this is my game, and I mean to play it well, because I love it! You can not let no person steal or take your love away. It's an art to this shit, and I plan to be the next Picasso in this shit. Only difference he was a painter, and I'm DJ, but music is an art also. This shit has to be put together in a certain way. For real!"

Hemi Entertainment begin using different advertising and marketing strategies to reach more people to perform various functions. They are rising like the sun when it breaks over or rises above the horizon that begins to shine. Plus, these are some cats with big dreams. RT said, "We have dreams, but we are <u>not</u> day-dreaming to where we are sleep walking. We are wide awake, and making moves to make those dreams a reality."

Next thing I started seeing various people with "*DJ RT Hemi Ent.*" on T-shirts. DJ RT Hemi told me has several ideas that he would not speak on concerning the Hemi Entertainment's future, and their plans for the next big step. I understood that, and definitely see the science of it. You can not speak about your dreams with everyone, because everyone don't want you to be successful. If you knew anything about Hemi Entertainment you would be just like me anticipating these brothers next move or function. Theses brothers just bring a certain energy that's genuine, and sincere when it comes to keeping their crowd on the floor. DJ RT is definitely correct when he stated that music is an art, and if you don't know how to create or paint that picture for your people, then you are in the wrong business. If you have not seen these brothers do their thing, then you are missing out. You can't ask a hater. If you do ask a hater, then know what to expect, and know why! The greater the hate, the more positive the thing is that the hater is hating.

"DJ RT Hemi Entertainment are on the rise, shining hard that it hurts you haters eyes. You can't stop the way we Swaggg and throw down, We're Swaggging hard and destine for our crown. Swaggging so hard through out the South, getting much love and our name keep flying out their mouths. We are on the rise, and we are coming alive, because we are in the swing of things, you can't stop this Swaggg regime.

Entertaining

What does it take to be an entertainer? It takes skills and dedication. What does it take to be skillful? Having that great love for what you love doing, and to become better. What does it take to be dedicated? Staying committed to the thing you love. This is what you see, you get and hear when Hemi Entertainment do their thing! The entertaining business is a tough business to be in, believe me, but the thing that makes it that much easier is dedication, skill and love. Without theses traits you can hang it up and forget about it. You have to be in the business for the long haul, and these brothers have been at it for years, and that's why they are making moves to carry them to the next level. The more people demand of you, the better you become, and the more you grow. When you cover all the twist and turns in the business, and stick with it. That means the people are getting what they pay for, and also they know they will have a damn good time! These brothers name and game has built them a rep that says, *"Swaggg and come shake that ass!!!"* DJ RT gave me a little input on what it takes to make money. He commented, "My brother told me it's several ways you can make big money, good money or get some money, but it depends on what you like or love, and are you willing to put in the time. Real-estate, feeding people, clothing people, selling transportation (car lot), owning or investing into insurance companies or oil companies (investing or part owner) or entertaining people by music, movies and books."

Three weeks had went by, and I haven't heard nothing from or about Hemi Entertainment doing anything. I know these guys wasn't going to let everything they worked hard for fall that easy, especially when you have spoken with these guys, and felt their energy. DJ RT wasn't answering his phones, he wasn't returning my emails, and wasn't even making statements and comments on Face-Book and Instagram. Still I wasn't getting any feedback. I was starting to think what did I do, that I shouldn't have done? Interviewing and talking with RT Hemi was the fuel that I needed that kept me going, and making certain business moves in my personal life. Entertaining was in this guy's blood and psychology for real. DJ RT probably didn't understand that I was getting my entertainment business lessons from chopping up with him. These guys carry an up-beat positive energy, that says I'm going to make it happen. They are personally energetic and contagious. The more I kick it with these young cats, the more it drives my desire for business. Anyway back to Hemi Entertainment that rose from plain Jane, to doing the damn thang!"

After those three long weeks went by slowly. I finally caught DJ RT Hemi and J-Boy, on the move they were headed back down deep South again after partying in a small town off Interstate-10. A few weeks later they were back in the "Ville" and before that Hwy-59 South numerous of times. These cats were back on the road. So at that moment I whipped my whip around, and started trailing these guys to the "Ville." I was really excited about talking with that damn DJ RT Hemi.

After what seem like hours we arrived at the spot. It was at a community place. That party was going down all that night. _No jive and no hype!!!_ It was hours later that I got the chance to chop it up with RT and J-Boy. I asked J-Boy, "What's be going on with Hemi Entertainment? I haven't heard anything from you guys. I haven't heard or seen any flyers about the next function. I was getting kind of depressed or worried for a moment?" J-Boy laughed heavily before he replied to my statement, "We always put out some type of info for people to know where and when we will get down! What town or city. Shit if we don't inform the people. How can we perform, and show them how we do it or where we do it. I don't know why you be missing out." J-Boy stepped back behind in the DJ's booth. I was waiting for the right time to speak with RT Hemi. This brother always had the fire of holding your attention, and making you wanting more of it. I don't know where he acquired that skill to hold you, and have you wanting more of his energy, wise words and great reasoning. This is baffling coming from a young man. I never talked with his mother, and his father had passed-on(may he R.I.P.). The only person I can think of was is brother P.Los. I just sat there sipping on a beer.

Dear reader, you not going to believe this when I make mention of it. Usually people would wait until they have had a few drinks before they consider dancing or asking someone to dance with them, but while we were down there in the "Ville", these people came through the door yelling, *"Lets party DJ RT, Lets party, Lets party DJ RT, Lets party!!!"* Right at that moment DJ RT switched the track before anyone knew what had happen. DJ RT Hemi put that whole crowd on the floor, every chair was empty except for mines, hah, hah!! I've never been a dancer, but I know good music when I hear it. Good music always makes you move. That floor was packed, and from that point on. I tell you what, that dance floor was not empty for once until we packed up, and got the hell out of there! Don't get me wrong, their were people taking a break from dancing too long, but the floor never stayed empty. While packing up, I must make mention that I helped pack up the equipment. That's when I got my few minutes with the man DJ RT Hemi. The spark within the flame, the fuel that enrages the fire, that dip in your hip, that groove in your dancing moves, and the juice that get you loose to bust a move or two. We embraced with that hood embracement, which goes back to our Ancestral lineage of Ancient Khemit now known has Egypt. I asked, "I haven't heard anything from RT Hemi Entertainment, and I asked J-Boy about that. I asked J-Boy, but he said you guys been on the move." He hit me, "For real, we been on the move to the "Seal to Da Ville" again. Shit I lost count of how many times we've been called back this way. This time we came back, because the word was getting around, and out in this "Ville" about us. That's what we want! People to give us a chance to see what we can and will do to ensure they have a good time. Plus, you will get your money's worth. I have been working on a few other things with my brother P. Los and with another influential guy, but I will not mention his name. I told you months ago stick with your boy, and you keep interviewing us. We are going to take you where we are trying to go, and that's on the next two levels. I'm not trying to sound boastful, or be egoistic or even macho. I don't like to reveal nothing I'm doing. I like to let my actions dictate what I'm doing. So let me say it this way, we are going to take over this South like a storm."

Taking Over The South Like A Storm

"The RT Hemi Entertainment are going to take the South by a storm, for real! I know you have heard me say that numerous of times. I only say this because of the plans, tactics and strategies that that I implement to do business," stated DJ RT Hemi. That were the words from that boy DJ RT Hemi. This brother would pop up on the scene for business, and after that it's like where did RT disappear to? I asked RT one night at one of their functions, why he just seems to disappear and this was his reply. "Why should any person stay on the scene all the time. That's when you began to be banal or stale to your people, then they start feeling apprehensive towards you. Next, your business begins to dwindle, and before you know it, you are out of business. If the business you say you love flops, that only means one or two things. One you went to sleep on the people and the business, and second you never did love the business in the first place. I love what I do, that's why I do it and do it like the people like for me to do."

I told DJ RT Hemi this one day when I was at the barber-shop. After getting my goatee trimmed. I asked DJ RT could I have a word with him outside. So we stepped outside, and these are the words I stated, "You noticed that things are changing around this town, and plus the neighboring cities and towns. Another thing that I think you should consider is the music world is changing also. Lets just focus on these little country towns that want people to DJ for them, and put their little town on the map and make money. Another thing to consider when you are negotiating with those country club owners. It's better tell them you can put their club and town on the map. Also inform them, that you can bring some action and business to their place of business if we can work on some form of contract. Give them some type of guarantee. Every man in business is in business to make money, so what you think?" DJ RT Hemi looked at me and smiled and said, "For real, but I'm a head of the game on that perspective. I got most these little towns on lock right now. Plus far as the music business, and the rap or hip-hop game. Shit I'm the future of hip-hop! Being in the business that I'm in, gives me a great edge on what's around and in that game. I don't like telling people my plans, because that goes against the art of winning. I'm slowing building on this business, and everything that comes with this Hip-Hop business. There are those pioneers that laid the foundation for Hip-Hop and d-jaying and when you watch and learn from those greats, you can only go higher. There are many Black pioneers of business that's important to my mindset of business and elevating. While they are getting older, the younger I'll still be in this game. I hope you got what I just said, about that age philosophy. Think about it?" I felt like I was helping, but this cat was ahead of the game. He's always thinking outside the box, like any good business person should think. Which is bigger, better, and smarter in order to maintain the business, and push the business forward to grow at all cost. In order for a business or any type of plan to grow big and be forceful like a storm, means that you have to be wisely aggressive, strategically prepared for the long haul, tacitly moving like a shark, and have your mindset on taking care of business. DJ RT stated, "Hemi Entertainment will be felt like a storm. Storm of parties, good music, creating and producing beats, and host of other things that I will not mention at this time! If, I am not felt by the people, then its not a storm at all. We will call it being under the weather." ha, ha [*laughing*]

RT Hemi told me one day in "Da Seal" a little town outside the big city of H-Town about the day when he got a call from his brother P. Los. They went to that same big house on the hill. Which was the home of P. Los' seminar business mentor and associate. DJ RT Hemi told me about that gray-gloomy day. "When we made it to that same house, and the same woman I had met, which was the wife that had let us in. Before entering

I notice that it was six or seven cars in the driveway when we first pulled up. You could tell that something wasn't right. His wife looked as though she have been crying. We followed her to this large bedroom. When we walked in, and there was that old wise business mentor and friend of my brother laying there looking sickly and weakly. It was hard to hear him, because he was so weak. He told everyone to leave the bedroom except my brother and me. These was his exact words, 'Hi, how are you gentlemen doing? P. Los, well my fellow brother you probably know why I have been pressing you to take care of my wife if something was to happen to me. I lost my son years ago from a bad car accident. That's why I started donating money to different charities for the homeless children, disease stricken kids, and education like colleges, but you both know about all that. I have been battling with this cancer thing for the past fifteen years, and this time it got the best of me. My fellow brother look in the closet to the right there, and look in that silk navy-blue smoking jacket, and there's a small gold key inside.' My brother walked in the closet, and moments later replied, 'I got it.' Then our mentor continued, 'Go all the way to the back of the closet to the right on the floor is a safe.' Minutes later my brother appeared coming out of the closet with a large blue folder. Then our mentor was coughing hard before he started talking again. He continued where he left off, 'My brother this for your brother, and a means to take his business to another level.' [*All laughing*] DJ RT Hemi, "I was afraid this guy might die on us, and I didn't want to see that, but that's part of life. You come in this world alive, but you got to leave here by dieing." Then our mentor replied, 'My brother you know what to do with that right?' DJ RT Hemi, "We all shook hands then we parted the bedroom, and the wife, the doctor, the sister of the wife, and few other that I have never seen went back into the bedroom. We sat down in this large living room, and the wife returned, and gave us both a hug, then we parted.

Later that week and the beginning of a new year my brother called me. He told me he got the news. Our mentor had passed on February 23, 2013. I knew right then and there at that point, I was going to always do me best. Here was a hard working man teaching me to work smart by investing and setting goals. Thanks to my brother P. Los, for introducing me to a world of business, goals, ambition, intelligence, strategic planning and most of all how to use a business like a Storm. It blows away bullshit, and rearranges things for a seasonal growth with a powerful reason by nature's great plan."

Swagggin for Life!!!!!!"

Swaggin On Them

Swagggin'

We Swagggin, never bragging,
About to cash in, and Paper stacking.
We Swagggin for sure,
Check out the dance floor,
Moving like the oceans waves from sea to sea,
You don't have to believe me just ask my peeps,
And hear the truth about who we be,
From city to city and town to town,
Everybody knows how we throw down,
Our parties are never a flop,
People shaking their asses and doing the bop,
Our game is sweet like the cream of the crop,
Haters are praying for us to flop,
But I think not, destine for the top,
The dance floor is never empty or needing a tune,
The way we Swaggg deliver the boom,
You are sure to be consumed by our tunes,
We enter the place with a certain swaggg,
That's serious about our name that engraves the tag,
For all my niggas get your cash,
Fuck the dumb shit that's the past,

We're moving like the speed of the light,
Throwing parties from the hottest to the coldest night,
Sipping cognac, beer and wine,
Everybody is having a damn good time,
Remember the rhyme.
We Swagggin, never bragging,
About to cash in and paper stacking.

Hustler Verbatim

It's the hustler's verbatim,
That got them suckers hating,
While them Hos are gyrating.

I'm another hustler with skills,
Moving from towns to cities on the real,
The name of the game is stack your chips,
Swerving in my whip,
Game keeps rolling off my tongue and lips,
Always on the move making deals,
And that's on the real,
Moving like twenty inch chromes wheels,
My verbal game keeps them suckers confused,
So they will never know my next move,
Sticking to the art of war, using tactics and strategies,
Stop trying to figure me out before your brain cells freeze,
Hitting them haters with an element of surprise,
Sticking to the rules of leaving you asking what and why,
All true hustlers wants and makes moves to have it all,
The cash, the homes, the cars and standing tall,
You haters are furious and wishing and hoping I'll fall,
I'm true to the universal rules and laws,,
When Karma hits your hating ass it fells like a chainsaw,
Your game is light like a feather,

And my verbatim blows like the Chi-town windy weather,
You suckers better get off me and leave me alone,
Before nature release her vengeful cyclone,
And when I truly spit this hustler shit,
Nine out of ten your will be in a mental twist.

Passing The Reigns

I'm passing the reigns,
Giving him the game,
Cause he's my son,
That's on the One.

As my son keeps getting older and the world is getting colder,
I'm putting in work to lighten his shoulders,
And I'm not sugar-coating nothing about life and how it's told,
I'm teaching him and telling him about life's dos and don'ts,
As he gets older he has to know about needs and wants,
I'm drillling him about haters and so-called friends,
How there's good and bad people that will do you end,
Watch out for them fake ass smiles and plastic grins,
I'm the King and he's the Prince,
Teaching him about the rules and laws of life's consequence,
I'm leaving him the true and real blue-print,
So he can build a bigger and better edifice from this,
One of the most important thing I express,
Telling him to always love his mom and show his pops respect,
I'm doing my best for my seed, family and me,
Taking and creating all types of opportunities,
Life is a game, so I'm passing him the reigns.

The Book Of Power

The Book of Power,
Is the words of the hour,
Listen to my prophecies,
About ambition and abilities.

Most you have not learned about hating,
It destroys you and keeps you waiting,
If you hate you can't learn,
So don't expect to earn,
Get ready for the fire of Hell and feel the burns,
Sitting and plotting like Satan,
Yes you with all your perpetrating and procrastinating,
For anyone that doesn't put in the lawful work,
You can't cheat the laws of the universe,
And you think that shit rightly suppose to work,
You get out what you put in,
Because in the end it's Satan and you desperate to win,
Stiff neck and rebellious to the truth,
Loving what's right and truth is the way fool,
Using the enemies tools to kill for rims and jewels,
You will pay the price with your life for breaking the rule,
Fuck all you slave minded ass niggers,
Not my real niggas that's putting in work for six figures,
But you devil minded hating suckers will get dealt with,
For all your hating, lies, and two-face tricks,
You can't be lazy and sitting around waiting and hating,
This is the Book of Power about ambition and elevating.

Conclusion

We finally come to concluded where there really isn't a conclusion for the Hemi Entertainment's future. There are many plans and future endeavors that DJ RT Hemi has in stored for his peeps, and those that love and support the Hemi Entertainment.

Also, there is many more things that the reader should greatly consider. How this book come to life right under many people's noses without them realizing what was really happening. This book came together like a good pot of gumbo. Once you had a taste(read it) you will take another taste(read it again). *"Anything that makes you feel good or that's good for you, can't be bad to you,"* as the old saying goes. The main thing that will puzzle many minds is how this work has come to life, and appear in your hands dear reader. I hope this mental business trip has been elating to you, as it has been for the RT Hemi Entertainment's present and future business missions. Now, there are many things that will be happening for the duration and future of Hemi Entertainment's continuation of good music, awesome parties, and many others things that I will not disclose to you at this time. Just keep your ears and eyes open for DJ RT Hemi Entertainment to swaggg with you.

Thanks

There are many people that the I, DJ RT Hemi would like to thank again. First foremost, I would like to thank our people that campaigned for me to do my thing, and I would like to thank those that has supported me throughout out the years.

I would like thank my mother, my son, my brothers, sister, and my nieces and nephews. I especially have to thank that boy P. Los. I would also like to thank my wife Lilly-Pad with her sweet support, believing in me and her encouragements. Got to give props to my boy "Skip The Barber" with clear cut sharp cutting with game. I like to thank them boys "B-2-da J" & (4 Dollaz). Last, but not least my nigga and ace J-Boy for having that fire and desire to Swaggg with me in the midst of so many haters and perpetrators. And my nigga with raw gutsy flows from the Lake, Ace Montana "Da hott-spitta." One Love from the Hemi Entertainment.

Suggestions

There are several books that I would like to encourge my readers to read, and for those that wish to be business owners or investors, and for any that wish to understand things of this present age that goes on behind the curtain of success, money and power.

Psychological Skullduggery:

*"In a world of manipulation, deceit, and
ruthlessness, is of the norm and all is fair play."*

This book, Psychological Skullduggery is book about having a certain mindest when it comes to business. Without a certain mindest for business you will never be in business. There is a mindset you must haveto begin or invest, to continue through all the short pitfalls, and grow mentally in order to handle many business situations like negotiating.

Political Veil: Positioning For Power

Learning and knowing how to politick is knowing the pecking-order of political-economics, comradeship, diplomacy and how Power is used and obtained.

<u>The Bitch Called Life</u>

This book about street hustling, learning human behavior, with a twist of mind games that has to be learned when it comes to hustling.

Another Book that I suggest you read:

<u>"Are You Loving What Is Not Loving You?"</u>

This book is about having a successful relationship, building relationships, changed lives, and saving marriages emotionally and economically.

By: Delady

You can purchase these books @ Author House.com & Amazon.com

One

Love

To

All

MY

Peeps!!!!!!!

Printed in the United States
By Bookmasters